The Table and the Chair

By Edward L

Illustrated by Jeff

Distributed by The Child's World®
1980 Lookout Drive • Mankato, MN 56003-1705
800-599-READ • www.childsworld.com

Acknowledgments
The Child's World®: Mary Berendes, Publishing Director
The Design Lab: Kathleen Petelinsek, Design

Library of Congress Cataloging-in-Publication Data
Lear, Edward, 1812–1888.
The table and the chair / by Edward Lear ; illustrated by Jeff Ebbeler.
p. cm.
ISBN 978-1-60973-156-4 (library reinforced : alk. paper)
1. Children's poetry, English. I. Ebbeler, Jeffrey, ill. II. Title.
PR4879.L2T33 2011
821'.8—dc22 2011005002

Printed in the United States of America in Mankato, Minnesota.
July 2011
PA02091

Said the Table to the Chair,
"You can hardly be aware,
how I suffer from the heat,
and from chilblains on my on my feet!

If we took a little walk,
we might have a little talk!
Pray let us take the air!"
said the Table to the Chair.

Said the Chair unto the Table,
"Now you know we are not able!
How foolishly you talk,
when you know we cannot walk!"

Said the Table, with a sigh,
"It can do no harm to try,
I've as many legs as you,
why can't we walk on two?"

So they both went slowly down,
and walked about the town
with a cheerful bumpy sound,
as they toddled round and round.

And everybody cried,
as they hastened to their side,
"See! The Table and the Chair
have come out to take the air!"

But in going down an alley,
to a castle in a valley,
they completely lost their way,
and wandered all the day.

Till, to see them safely back,
they paid a Ducky-quack,
and a Beetle, and a Mouse,
who took them to their house.

Then they whispered to each other,
"O delightful little brother!
What a lovely walk we've taken!
Let us dine on beans and bacon!"

So the Ducky, and the leetle browny-Mousy and the Beetle dined, and danced upon their heads till they toddled to their beds.

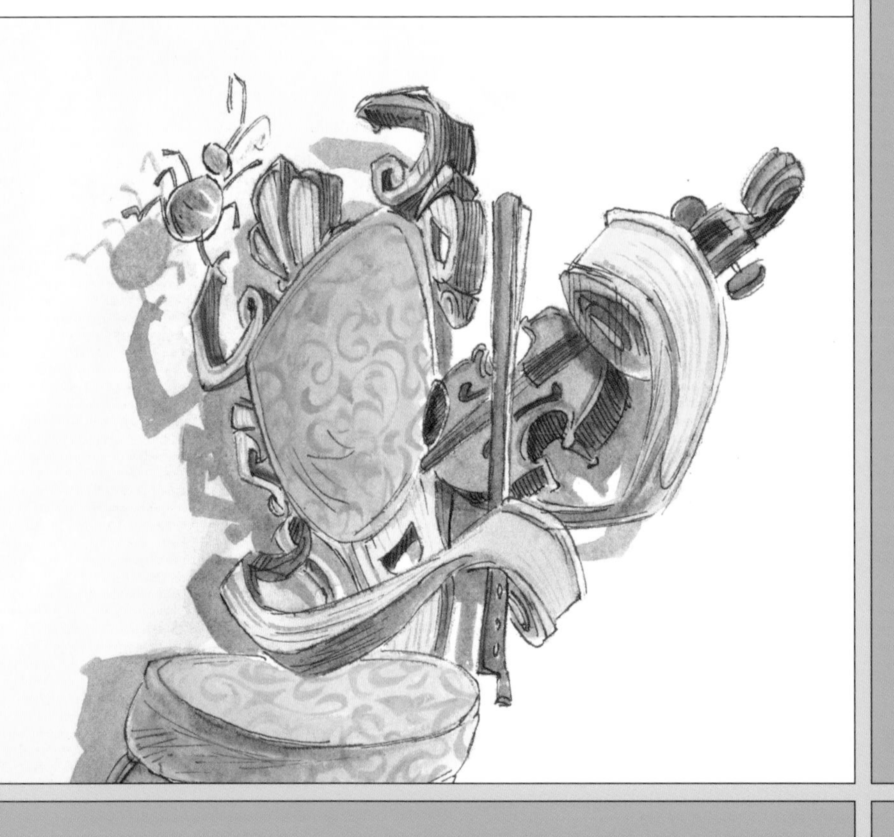

The Table and the Chair

Said the Table to the Chair,
"You can hardly be aware,
how I suffer from the heat,
And from chilblains on my on my feet!
If we took a little walk,
We might have a little talk!
Pray let us take the air!"
Said the Table to the Chair.

Said the Chair unto the Table,
"Now you know we are not able!
How foolishly you talk,
When you know we cannot walk!"
Said the Table, with a sigh,
"It can do no harm to try,
I've as many legs as you,
Why can't we walk on two?"

So they both went slowly down,
And walked about the town
With a cheerful bumpy sound,
As they toddled round and round.

And everybody cried,
As they hastened to their side,
"See! The Table and the Chair
Have come out to take the air!"

But in going down an alley,
To a castle in a valley,
They completely lost their way,
And wandered all the day.
Till, to see them safely back,
They paid a Ducky-quack,
And a Beetle, and a Mouse,
Who took them to their house.

Then they whispered to each other,
"O delightful little brother!
What a lovely walk we've taken!
Let us dine on Beans and Bacon!"
So the Ducky, and the leetle
Browny-Mousy and the Beetle
Dined, and danced upon their heads
Till they toddled to their beds.

—Edward Lear

What makes a poem a poem?

With just a few words, a poem can make you feel things in a flash. It delights you, amazes you. It makes you laugh out loud or shed a tear. You know a poem is successful when it tickles your brain or touches your heart.

Poets choose their words very carefully. They don't just think about what words *mean.* They think about how they *sound.* Why write "sticky mess," when "mashed marshmallow" is so much more fun to say? Those repeating *m* sounds? They're alliteration in action!

Poets surprise you with similes and metaphors. A school hallway becomes a pirate's plank. A bed flies away in a dream. In this way, poets make their words come alive. A poem about a campfire makes you wrinkle your nose. A poem about a slithering snake makes you squirm in your seat.

Poets have all kinds of tools and tricks to make their work come alive. Maybe it's a rhyming verse. Maybe it's the rhythm of repeated sounds. Maybe it's the imagery of a melting ice cream cone. With the tricks of the trade, anything can become a poem!

About the Author

Edward Lear was a famous writer, poet, and artist. He was born in England in 1812. Lear was a skilled painter, and he most enjoyed painting birds or nature scenes. He is best known for his poems, called *limericks*, which were often about silly things and magical creatures. Lear died in 1888.

About the Illustrator

Jeffrey Ebbeler has been creating award-winning art for children for almost a decade. He has illustrated more than 40 picture books. He has also done paper engineering for pop-up books, created large scale murals for schools and churches, and sculpted puppets and performed for several marionette theaters. He and his wife currently live in Cincinnati with their twin daughters.